AF291516

Queen of the Negev

An Inspirational Photo Story

Mark Kotzen

Queen of the Negev
An Inspirational Photo Story

ISBN 978-965-599-850-4

Mark Kotzen can be contacted at
moshe@photomark.pics

Revivim
40
224
Dimona Junc.
Efe Mnt.
Rotem Fertilizers
Zafit Junc.
Zeya'im Mnt.
Hamarmar Mnt.
Sedom
Mnt. Keren
Mash'abim Junc.
Mashabe Sade
204
Yeroham Junc.
204
206
Rotem Mnt.
25
Arnon
Hatzeva Junc.
Holot Shunera
Givat Hayal
Ashalim
211
Telalim Junc.
Telalim
Yeroham
225
Hamahtesh Hagadol
227
Mizpe Hamahtesh
Hamahtesh Hakatan
Phosphate Plant
Ein-Tamar
Nezer Mnt.
Mnt. Rechama
204
Mnt. HaTira
Oron
Karbolet
Mezad Zafit
Mezad Aqrabim
Shdemot Shizaf
Mitzpeh Shivta
211
Givot Mesura
Halukim Junc.
Sde Boker
206
Golehan Mnt.
Hahalak Mnt.
Zin Phosphate Plant
227
Raviv Mnt.
Nezer Mnt.
Boqer Mnt.
Midreshet Ben-Gurion
Zaror Mnt.
Givat Mador
Rekhev Mnt.
Midbar Zin
Hatzeva
Rut Mnt.
Ziporim Junc.
Ben-Gurion Tomb
Rahamim Mnt.
40
Horvot Avedat
Orahot Mnt.
I'Ovot
Ein Hatzeva Junc.
Ein Hatzeva
Idan
Lavan Mnt.
Argov Mnt.
Eldad Mnt.
Aqev Mnt.
H A N E G E V
Rasisim Mnt.
Teref Mnt.
Marzeva Mnt.
90
Hatzeva
Hamran Mnt.
Qemer Mnt.
Nafha Mnt.
850
Sa'ad Mnt.
Gerfaon Mnt.
Enmar Mnt.
Enmar
Dohan
Ayarim Mnt.
Agrab Mnt.
Ayarim
Haruhot Junc.
Mezad Mahmal
Ardon Mnt.
Mnt. Yahav
Ein Yahav
Hemet Mnt.
Mizpe Ramon
Haminsara Visitors Center
Mezad Mishor
Gizron Mnt.
171
Mahtesh Ramon
Sappir
Gevim Mnt.
Darga Mnt.
Pitam Mnt.
Govay Mnt.
Tzofar
Omer Mnt.
Ramon
Oded Mnt.
1000
Keinan
Ma'ale Hameishar
Harif Mnt.
Makhbir Mnt.
Mahane Zofar
Zofar
Loz Mnt.
Qirton Mnt.
Hameshar Mnt.
Nishpe Mnt.
Ramat Zofar
120
Mnt. Me'ara
Arif Mnt.
40
Kippa Mnt.
Batur Mnt.
Hisun Mnt.
Mazer
Re'im
Barag
Nes Mnt.
Mnt. Sagi
Mikha'el Mnt.
Karkom
Paran
Ma'ale Paran
Eshet Mnt.
96

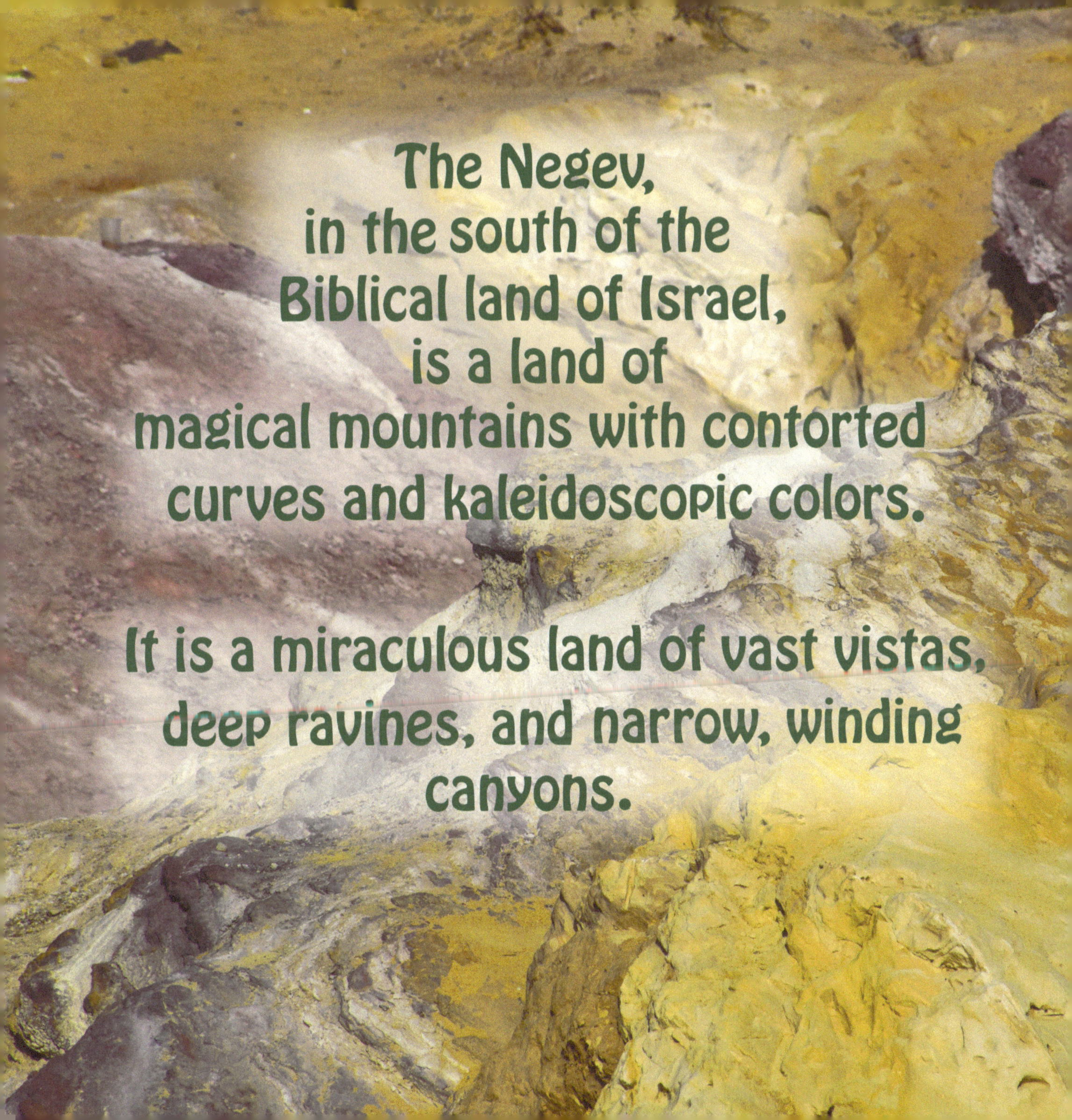

The Negev,
in the south of the
Biblical land of Israel,
is a land of
magical mountains with contorted
curves and kaleidoscopic colors.

It is a miraculous land of vast vistas,
deep ravines, and narrow, winding
canyons.

A noble Queen rules the Negev desert.
Most of the time, life is calm – besides the
occasional drought, flood and other
miscellaneous annoyances.
"If one waits long enough any problem will
 resolve itself."
This has been the Queen's chosen method
of governing, and a rather successful
method at that. After all, when your time
frame is near to eternity (however long
that is), a mere five-year drought is a drop
(or a missing drop) in the bucket of time.
Even humankind's constructive and
destructive activities don't last longer
than a century or two.

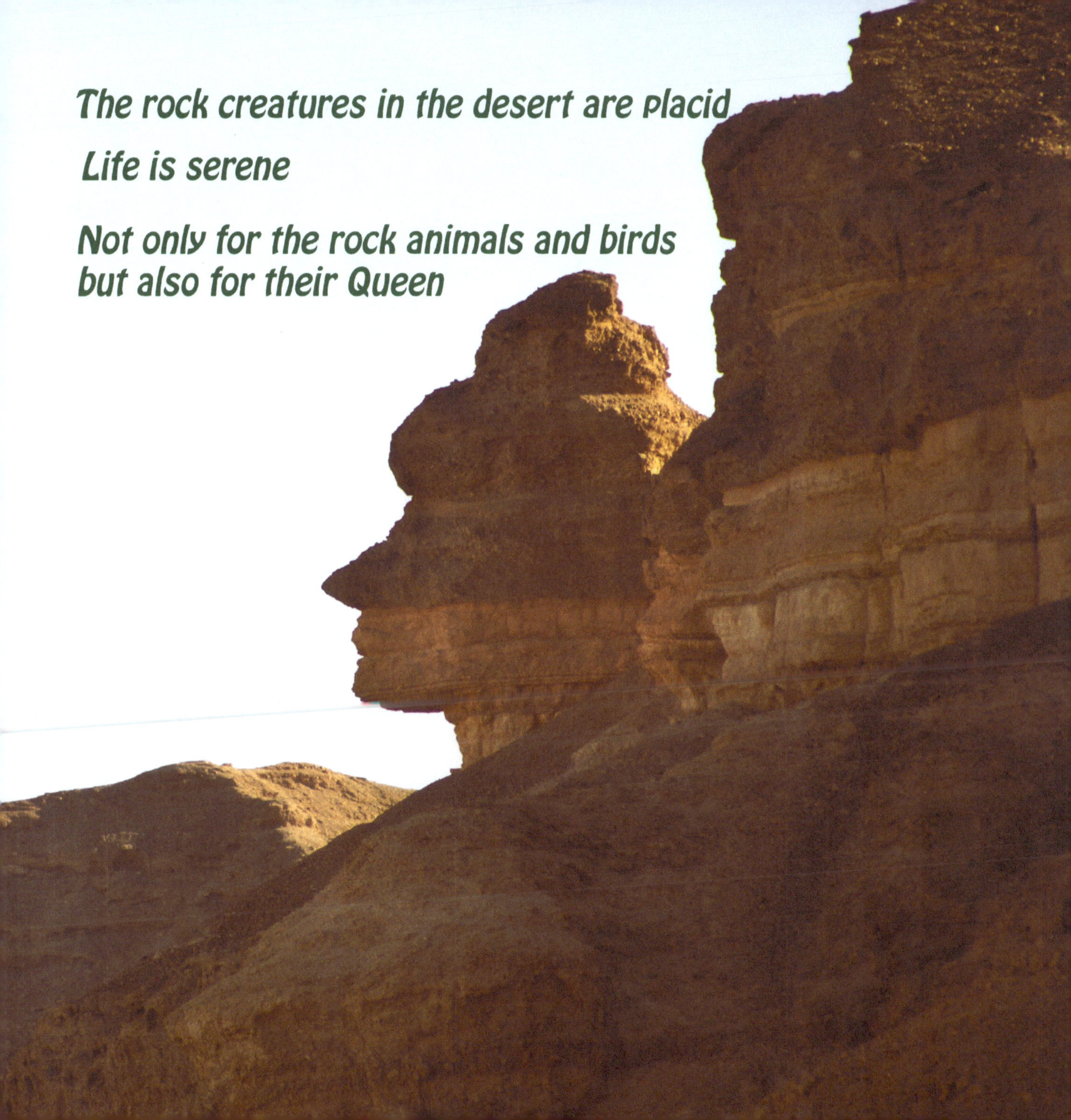
The rock creatures in the desert are placid

Life is serene

Not only for the rock animals and birds
but also for their Queen

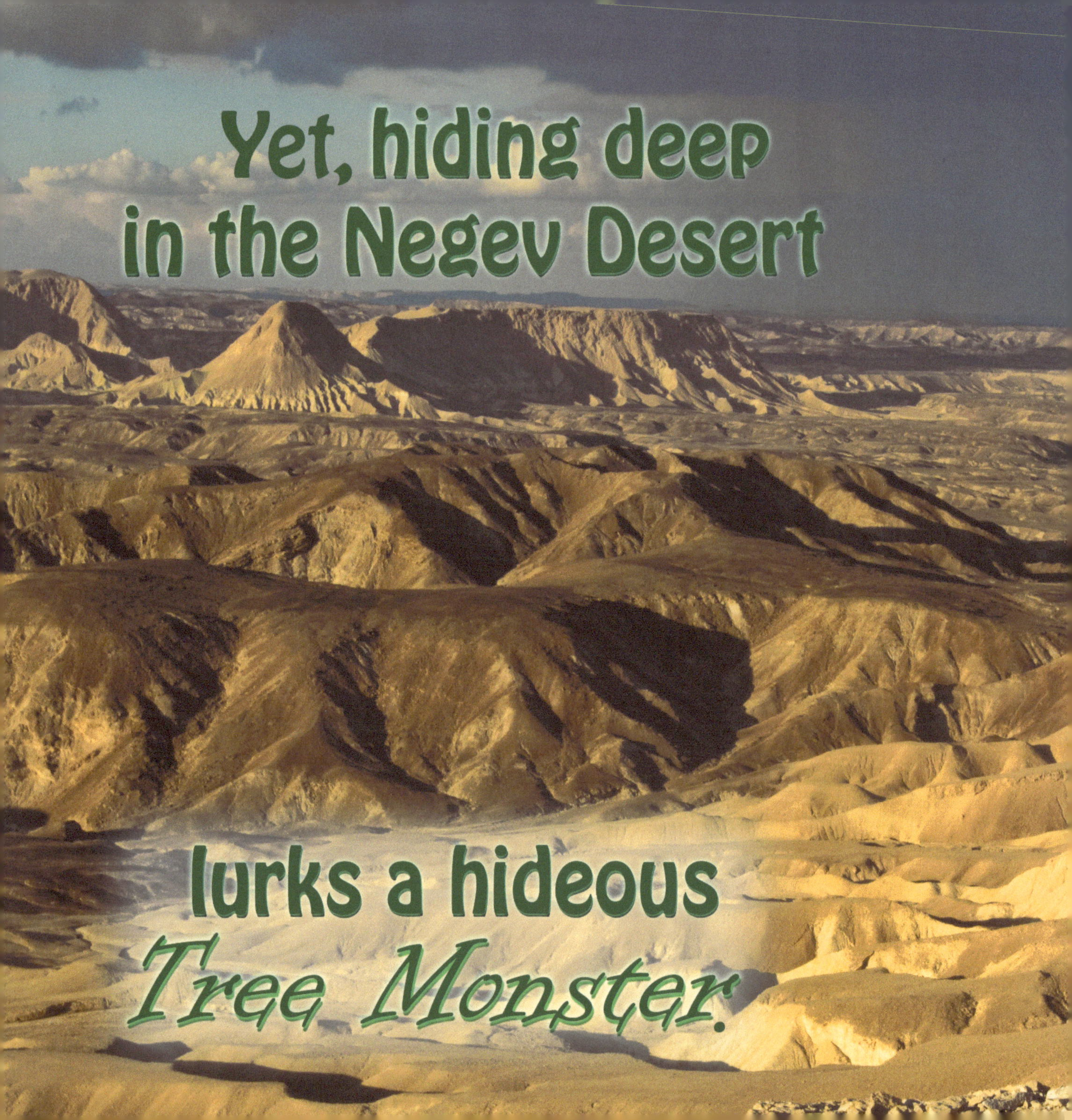
Yet, hiding deep
in the Negev Desert

lurks a hideous
Tree Monster.

The Tree Monster
is part of the
Master Plan.

The rocks and their Queen are blissfully unaware of the *Tree Monster*'s presence, and life continues as usual. The rocks in the Queendom do not move much. They stick faithfully to their posts, even when battered by hot winds and sandstorms. While they do get tossed about during the occasional flash floods, they are generally well-balanced and supportive of one another.

Despite staying put, they are never bored
After all, they reside in the house of the Lord

By and large, they feel safe and sound
Every rock and pebble holds its ground

The rocks have a carefree approach to life.
They are not given to introspection. They take
life as it comes. Whether a rock-bird perched on
a cliff, or some other unnamed rock animal, they
have no possessions. Neither do any of the rocks
nearby. Nor are there any territorial ambitions
because nothing goes anywhere. With nothing to

incite jealousy, the rocks are inexperienced in overcoming envy. They have nothing about which to argue, and so never learned the art of conflict resolution. Not much incentive for self-development here.

Yet God, Creator of the rocks, does indeed expect something from them. They have no need to joust jealousy or contain conflict. However, He wants them to be thankful to Him for their existence – to look Heavenward. They were created as awe-inspiring creatures in the Holy Land, and they, in turn, are expected to nurture a growing connection with their Creator – to broaden their understanding of His ways.

God decides change is needed. It is time to implement the *Master Plan.*

Meanwhile, the Queen sits
with passive peaceful poise,
savoring the sunset.

One fine day, the Queen spots something
far off in the distance... could it be? A hideous
creature lurking – the *Tree Monster.* Not since the
great earthquake several centuries past, has the
Queen been so *shaken*. Even a bolder boulder than
the Queen herself would have been bowled over.

The *Tree Monster* is a sight awful to behold –
 Especially for a Rock Queen not very bold

The Queen is hopelessly afraid –
 She is in desperate need of aid

True, the monster is but a tree –
    Yet *she* is but a rock –
And sometimes it is the tree that wields
more power than the rock.

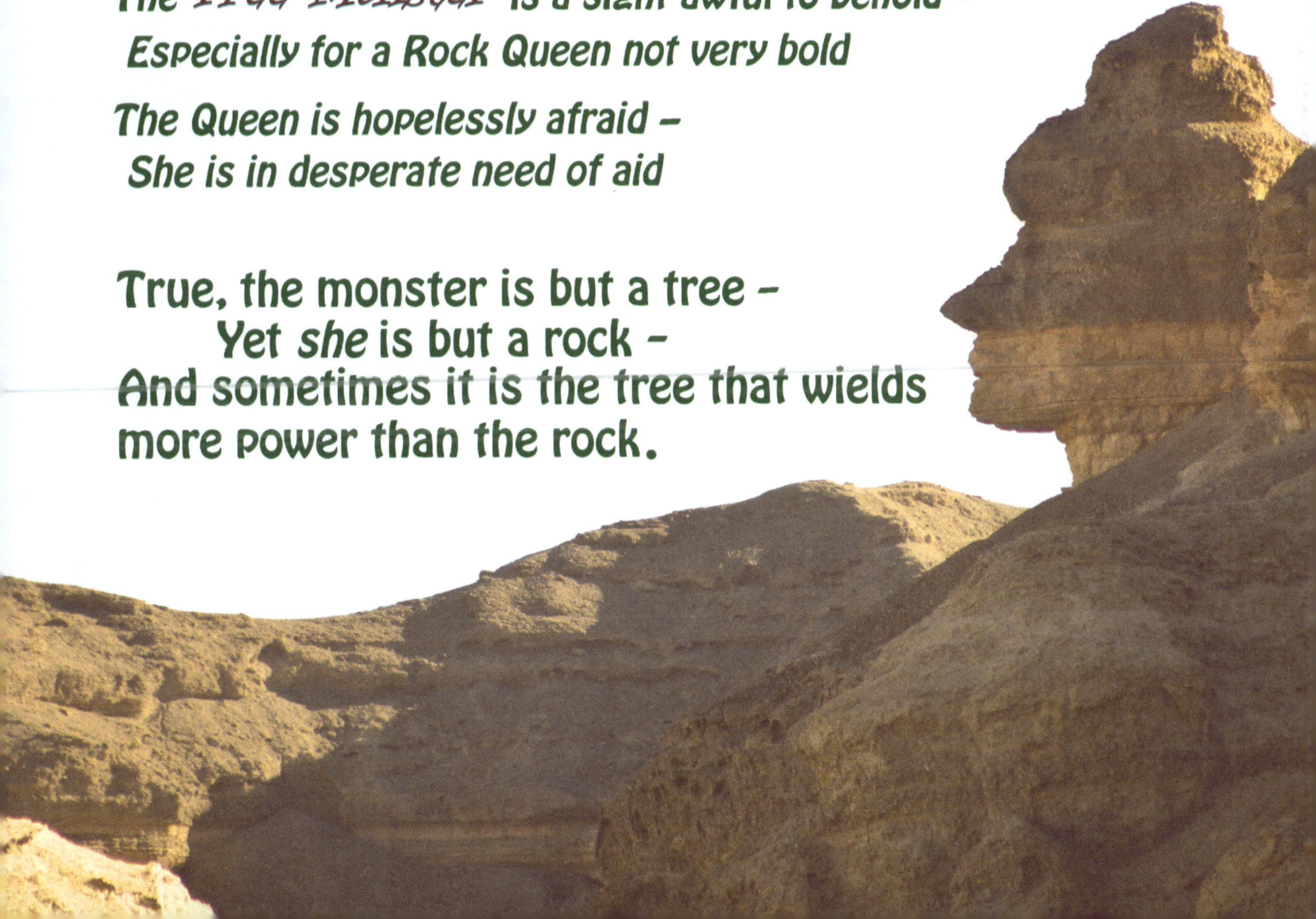

It starts in a teeny-tiny crack,
and grows and grows—
pushing *splitting* *cra-a-acking*

True, the Tree Monster may seem quite benign.
But the Queen realizes that destruction is just
a matter of time. The Monster could squeeze through
rock with the cunning of a fox—and the strength of an ox.

What can be done?
There is nowhere to run
They cannot flee the tree
In any case, it is not a fair race
The Queen's subjects are stuck in their place

She feels helpless and hopeless,
more of a wreck than a rock.

The Queendom, of course, has its own Tree Dog. However, there is no way the Tree Dog could fight the *Tree Monster*. Though they are both trees, they are dissimilar as chalk and cheese.

The Tree Dog is very cute and never grows. He jibes perfectly with the rocks, unambitious and unchanging. True, he has plenty of bark but no bite.

The *Tree Monster*'s bulging, on the other hand, is scary. He craves expansion. He breaks the rocks and casts them aside. He might even topple the Queen herself. She would roll far, far down to the deep gorge below, probably breaking her pointy nose along the way. Even if she would survive the fall unscathed, she could not possibly reign from there.

Her subjects would be ruled by a dictator. What can be done?

The age-old strategy of "waiting it out" will not work.

The *Tree Monster* threatens. The Queen has to protect her cities—

the stores and malls,
the hospitals and halls,
the houses and churches,
the birds' peepholes and perches,
the synagogues and mosques,
the cafes and kiosks.

All are in danger and look to their Queen for protection.
Will she save them?
Can she ward off this formidable foe?

To whom can she turn?
Her Turtle is truly a brave animal, as tough as rock. He stood his ground during a flood several decades past. Heroically, he protected the small stones that clung to him, saving them from being swept into oblivion.

But still, he is no match for a *Tree Monster*. He is much too small to defeat such a terrible and beastly foe. There has to be some solution out here somewhere.

The Queen's subjects are afraid to leave their caves to tend to their gardens. They risk being crushed by the *Tree Monster*.

The Negev is a place with a big heart
Now it is in danger of falling apart
It's obvious that they are under attack—
The only question is how to fight back
The Queen feels tired

Perhaps it is time for the Queen to take a rest. For how many centuries can she be expected to protect everyone? A rock, no matter how royal, needs time for itself. She wants to be a good rock *and roll* with the punches. But perhaps she can take some time out? She longs to simply ride the elevator UP UP UP UP UP

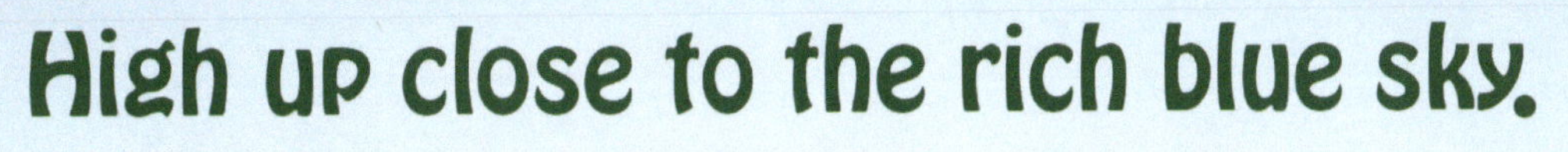

High up close to the rich blue sky.

All the way up to her castle
To settle down without hassle
Admitting to being vulnerable
She might as well get comfortable
Would it be so clearly wrong
To hide in the castle all day long?

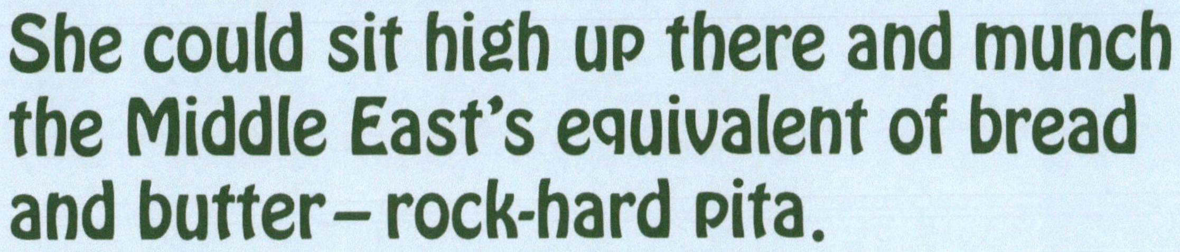

She could sit high up there and munch the Middle East's equivalent of bread and butter – rock-hard pita.

SHE KNOWS THAT IN THE LANDS OF MEN EATING IS OFTEN USED AS A REMEDY FOR HARDSHIP. THE QUEEN IS NOT CONVINCED THAT MANKIND'S IDEAS ARE GOOD.

She remembers what happened a while back in the great and fertile valley of Sodom and Gomorrah.

The Queen was too far away to see what occurred, but news traveled. The humans did not behave nicely at all. Man's approach to life caused a humanitarian and environmental disaster. The once lush valley became a totally Dead Sea. Not even fit for fish. Fish? No *plant* could survive in the super-salty water. Although it's rumored that overweight humans enjoy temporary weightlessness by floating in the dense, mineral-rich sea.

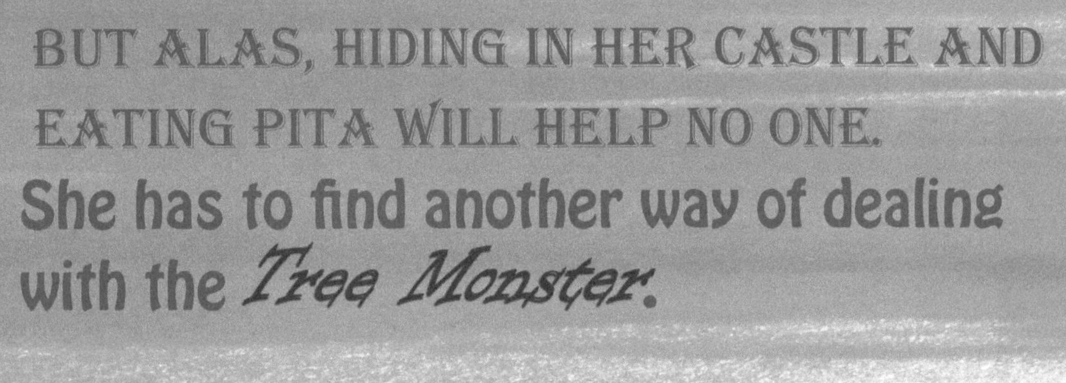

BUT ALAS, HIDING IN HER CASTLE AND
EATING PITA WILL HELP NO ONE.
She has to find another way of dealing
with the *Tree Monster.*

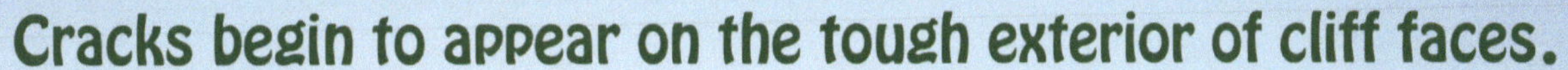

Cracks begin to appear on the tough exterior of cliff faces.

What is a rock to do against the *pushing* *splitting* and *cra-a-acking* of a *Tree Monster*? Gloom descends on the land. Rocks begin to despair. The future is uncertain. How many more centuries can they endure before the cruel *Tree Monster* will shove them brutally aside?

The end is near
A land in fear
Rocks losing hope
The Queen cannot cope
This catastrophe surpassed
Any threat from the past

The Queen's sad gaze passes over the land. She sees a rock's eye shed a rocky teardrop. At that sight she hits rock bottom.

All is lost.

Suddenly, out of the depths of despair, comes a flash of inspiration. That's it! She overlooked the obvious. How could she have been so hard-headed? She had forgotten God! She became comfortable sunning herself and enjoying the view – without thanking the Creator of the view. Hers is a faulty attitude that ought to be filled with gratitude. It is downright rude. The Lord should be adored instead of ignored.

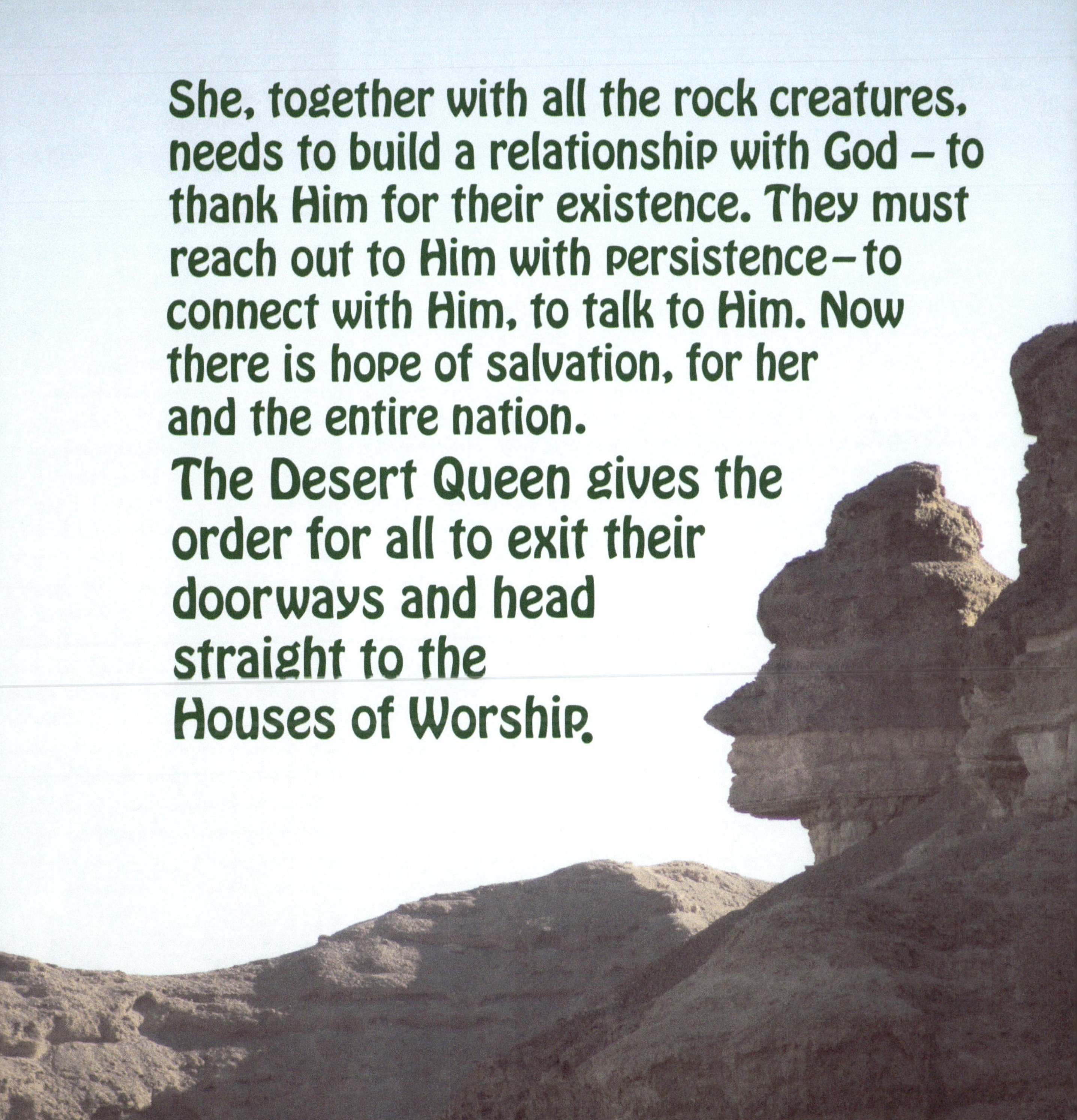

She, together with all the rock creatures, needs to build a relationship with God – to thank Him for their existence. They must reach out to Him with persistence – to connect with Him, to talk to Him. Now there is hope of salvation, for her and the entire nation.

The Desert Queen gives the order for all to exit their doorways and head straight to the Houses of Worship.

The Houses of Prayer quickly fill up.
Rocks stand outside,
pressing against the walls.

The churches, temples, synagogues, and mosques are all full to bursting. Congregations are thirsting for God. They beg that their pleas be heard. They realize they have strayed, so they pray and pray. They determine to change. Tears flow and soften their hearts, as they resolve to be happy, thankful rocks. They cry so moistly that their hearts become soggy.

The rocks are responding splendidly to the message of the Tree Monster. They are working toward a bond with God. The Tree Monster is no longer needed, so God turns it into a a grumpy but harmless Rock-Man. He remains so to this day.

It is unusual for a tree to become a rock, so it is called a miracle. The Queen and her subjects continue to strengthen their bond with their Creator. As for the Rock-Man, he sits in silence, a quiet reminder that

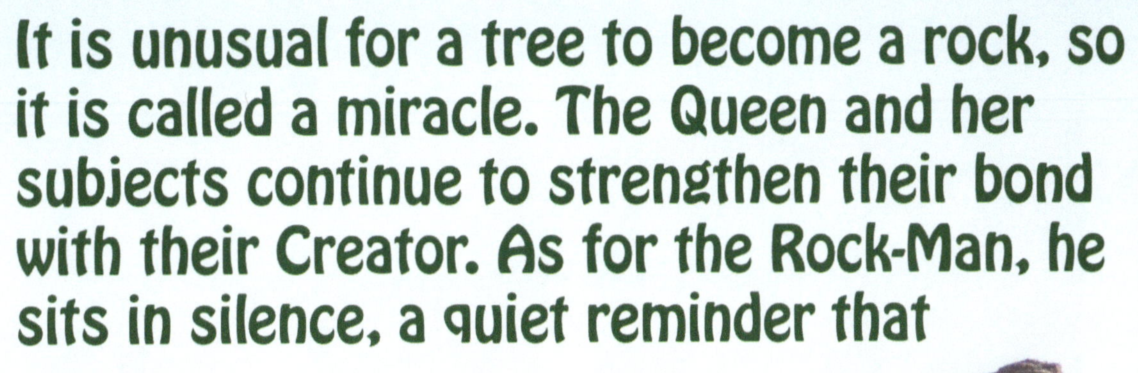

when stone hearts turn soft, you can expect a miracle.

Where we hang out.
Nachal Paran
Ramon Crater

Mt. Amir
Maale Zeelim & Akrabim
Nachal Meitzar
Note:
The word nachal translates somewhat optimistically as "river." Almost every nachal in the Negev is a dry riverbed.

In truth,
the Negev
also has a
King.
That is a whole different story.

Ingram Content Group UK Ltd.
Milton Keynes UK
UKHW050238220423
420605UK00003B/33